Playground Games and Skills

J. Robert Frith
Physical Education Adviser
Hampshire County Council

and Rowland Lobley
Physical Education Adviser
Buckinghamshire County Council

A & C Black Ltd
London

A & C Black Ltd
4 Soho Square
London WIV 6AD

© A & C Black 1971

First printed 1971
ISBN 0 7136 1162 6

Made and printed in Great Britain by
Billing & Sons Limited, Guildford and London

PLAYGROUND GAMES
AND SKILLS

Contents

Acknowledgements

Patrick J. Gillespie, Physical Education Organiser, Sunderland, for supplying the Foreword and for early inspiration;

Robert Pettigrew, Outdoor Pursuits Adviser, Hampshire, for all photographic contributions;

R. M. Marsh, M.A., County Education Officer, Hampshire, for permission to take and reproduce photographs of pupils, facilities and equipment in Hampshire schools;

The head teachers of the following Hampshire Schools, for permission to work with their pupils and to take and reproduce photographs:

Bishops Waltham, Ridgemede School
Chandlers Ford, Fryern Junior School
Romsey County Junior School
St Peter's R.C. School, Winchester
Wildground Junior School, Dibden Purlieu

All the *children* who have aided the production of this book in so many ways and their *parents* who have permitted them to stay after school to help.

Foreword

Patrick J. Gillespie, Physical Education Organiser, Sunderland

Teachers in primary schools who are concerned with the process of keeping abreast of developments in all the different subjects which they are required to teach will find this work of inestimable benefit. It has been prepared by two people who have a keen awareness of the rightful place of physical education in the development of younger children, and who recognise the importance of associating enjoyment with learning.

The various games which are suggested by the authors have obviously been carefully chosen both for their educational value and for the ease with which they can be taught in primary schools by those members of staff who have had no specialised training in this field. It is obvious that the authors have studied the subject in depth and tried out their ideas with primary school children to ensure that each activity fulfils the purpose which it is designed to serve.

The book, however, has a wider appeal than to practising teachers in primary schools. Organisers and inspectors will find it well worthy of their perusal. More particularly, it should prove of great value to both staff and students in colleges of education.

Introduction

This book is offered as a simple guide, for the benefit of primary school teachers and teachers in training who have neither a technical knowledge of games nor specialised training in the coaching of games.

Although reference is sometimes made in the following chapters to coaching techniques employed in various games, no individual game is dealt with in depth. On the contrary, a wide range of games is considered, offering the teacher a variety of interesting activities, through which his pupils might explore many enjoyable aspects of learning.

The main emphasis of this book is not upon games themselves, but upon the requirements of the children and the means by which these requirements can be satisfied.

I Aims

The playing of games is an essential part of a child's development, and even without the help and guidance of teachers, children will play games, because they enjoy doing so. At primary school level, the more popular games are those which involve a good deal of active physical participation. Without doubt, enjoyment and exercise are major features of games at this age level.

One cannot doubt the educational merit of developments in gymnastics in the primary school during the last decade. Through educational gymnastics, children learn to manage their body weight and to acquire skill through exploration and through meeting a variety of challenges in changing circumstances. In similar fashion, games situations provide fertile ground for the growth of learning.

Within the framework of the broad aims of education, the general aims of games in the primary school can be summarised as follows:

Enjoyment.
Exercise.
The opportunity to acquire skill.

Children enjoy those activities from which they get rewarding experiences; these experiences are worth much consideration, since they are basic essentials of the primary school games period.

Achievement is, perhaps, the most gratifying of these experiences. The well-worn cliché that 'Success breeds success' is particularly true of primary school games. Children should be presented with opportunities for success, no matter how low their level of skill may be, and, in this respect, the games must be adjusted to accommodate all children as will be illustrated in succeeding chapters.

Variety is another factor which widens the base of a child's experience, and helps him to become selective.

Initiative is encouraged by the presentation of opportunities for a child to select activities, apparatus and solutions to problems posed.

Responsibility can be both collective and individual. Group membership imposes its own responsibilities: children should be encouraged to accept responsibility for their personal clothing and footwear, and for the games apparatus used by the class or group. Moreover, opportunities for children to create rules for games enhance their feeling of responsibility.

These factors are part of learning and also add to the enjoyment, and with enjoyment comes more active participation and an increase in activity associated with a rise in the level of attainment. In other words, skills tend to be acquired and improved upon. Clearly, then, the basic aims are interrelated and always evident in the successful games lesson.

Children should not be obliged to play games which are beyond their capabilities when there are so many worthwhile alternatives. For example, the traditional game of cricket is most unsuitable for a majority of primary school children. A game played over successive weeks may only give each player the opportunity to have one innings. This opportunity to wield a bat is often terminated by one ball or very few balls. For many batsmen, the enjoyment factor is thus reduced to a minimum, exercise is almost non-existent, and this can hardly be regarded as an opportunity to acquire skill, but perhaps even worse is the frustration, which could result in apathy or even opposition to a fine national game. Participation for the fielders is limited to the times when the ball comes within fielding distance; at other times, fielding becomes a spectator role. Few primary school children have a knowledge of cricket tactics. Without this knowledge, enjoyment of the spectator role is limited to team partisanship. Bowlers are usually chosen from the select few who are capable of bouncing a ball in the vicinity of the wicket. Equipment for cricket, even that designated as junior equipment, is often unsuitable for many primary school children. Bats are often too heavy, pads too cumbersome and the pitch too long, and some children are afraid of the hard cricket balls.

In spite of all this, cricket can offer splendid opportunities for young children to enjoy themselves, and to get exercise and skill, if the game is carefully adapted. Skills like batting, bowling, throwing and catching can be practised with more suitable equipment, in simplified form, employing smaller groups of children, and with frequent repetitions. These practices include the playing of actual games.

The comments above can quite reasonably be applied to most major national games, which have evolved as adult pastimes with complex rules, large playing areas and bulky apparatus.

In any ball game involving twenty-two players over a period of, say, forty minutes, the average contact between each player and the ball must be under two minutes. When one considers the time absorbed by stoppages and the time the ball is outside the playing area, this contact period is probably reduced to a little over one minute. For some people, particularly in the primary school, the contact period could well be reduced to nil. While it is true that some players exercise their skill 'off the ball', it is also true that many more players at primary school level exercise skill only when they are actually playing the ball. Consequently, the playing of a national game, while often an enjoyable exercise, is hardly an economic method of furthering education through the medium of games.

The teacher can help children to learn and, at the same time, can help them to enjoy major and national games by presenting opportunities for practice of skills in such a way that the less able pupils are enabled to participate fully, while the more able pupils are encouraged to increase and extend their ability through more frequent repetitions than they might obtain in actually playing those games. In order to present these opportunities, the teacher should resort to games and practices which involve small groups of children, working within confined spaces. The games should involve a high frequency of scoring, offering all children opportunities for success.

2 Organisation and planning

In the preceding chapter, it was suggested that children should be arranged in small groups for the playing of games. The way in which the groups are formed will be determined largely by the age of the children concerned, their total number, the available space and the available apparatus.

For lower juniors, and certainly for infants, grouping according to sex is entirely unnecessary. In the upper part of the junior school, it is sometimes advisable to have groups consisting entirely of boys or entirely of girls. This is because boys' and girls' techniques in the playing of many games tend to develop, quite naturally, along different lines. However, this segregation should not be enforced unnecessarily, as there is a good deal of social merit in mixed games.

If there is an abundance of space available, it may be possible to divide a class into eight groups, each group containing four or five children. However, in many primary schools, the available space, particularly space on a hard surface, often does not exceed the area of one netball court, i.e., 100 ft by 50 ft or 30·48 m by 15·24 m. Under these circumstances, a more suitable arrangement is that of six groups with approximately six children to a group.

Each group should be responsible for its own comprehensive range of small apparatus. This apparatus is kept in a wire storage basket or box. The former is more suitable as it is usually lighter than a box, more durable and its contents can be viewed more readily. Ideally, the basket should have a handle at each end so that two small children can easily carry it between them. The wire should be galvanised or plastic coated and the basket should measure approximately 70 cm in length, 36 cm in width and 30 cm in depth. Partitions are not desirable, as they prevent the accommodation of such items as shinty sticks and cricket bat shapes (plate 3). The baskets each have a card attached to one end or side. At the top of this card is the name or number of the group responsible for the basket. Group names like 'Panthers' or 'Swallows' may be selected by the children, so long as these names are acceptable to similar groups in other classes. If the cards are of different colours, this is a further aid to recognition and children often enjoy decorating these cards to distinguish them still further.

There are several advantages to the basket system. One of them is that the children are encouraged to accept responsibility. At the beginning of the period, each group leader should check the contents of his or her basket against a detailed list of these contents, which should be printed on the card below the name or number of the group, and any additional or missing items are reported to the teacher who can then rectify the matter before work begins. At the end of the period, group members return their apparatus to the baskets and the group leader checks as before; again, any additional or missing items should be brought to the teacher's notice without his having to check each piece of equipment, and so he saves a considerable amount of time. Each basket is allocated a position on the perimeter of the playing area so that it forms a collecting point for the group concerned.

The basket may also be utilised as a stabiliser for a high jump stand, as illustrated in chapter 3.

The playing area for games is usually a playground, a grass surface or the floor of a hall. However, the hall floor is not normally suitable, lending itself more readily to gymnastics and dance, and it should only be used for games if long periods of bad weather have made playing out of doors impossible. Apart from the obvious limitations in the choice of the games to be played, the restricted floor area does not permit maximum participation by all children.

Most of the primary school, small-group games can be played either on a grass area or on a hard surface playground, the softer surface of the former being more suitable for games and practices associated with athletics, and the grass surface also tends to be larger than a playground, allowing more space for games which require an extensive area. However, there is a good deal to be said for limiting the playing space and thus increasing the intensity of the games being played. In most cases, the playground also offers a faster, truer surface.

As suggested earlier, the playing area might be limited to one netball court, in which case groups can be arranged with their baskets as illustrated in plate 4 and figure 1. A netball court, 30·48 m by 15·24 m, is divided into three sections which provide equal courts or games areas. If more than one netball court is available, this will obviously increase the number of pitches. If the available space is greater than the area of one netball court, certain activities may take place outside the three small pitches.

However, the netball court forms a good assembly area and places the children within satisfactory vocal range of the teacher.

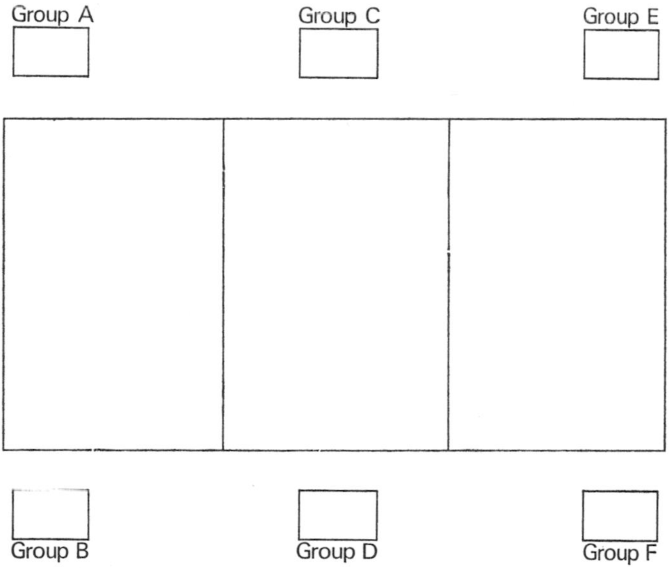

Group A   Group C   Group E

Group B   Group D   Group F

figure 1

The pitches illustrated in figure 1 can be used for games played end to end. For example, group A may play group B in a game of skittle ball, while, simultaneously, group E may play group F in a game of captain ball. These games are explained in chapter 6.

It is also possible, with the aid of playground chalk, to sub-divide a pitch into smaller areas or courts like those required for volleyball and tennis type games (figure 2). In this case, while groups A, B, E and F are playing five or six per side team games, group C might be divided on either side of a high net for Newcombe or quoit tennis. In the meantime, group D may be indulging in tennis type activities over a low net or practising athletic activities in the remaining space.

Figure 2 suggests one possible arrangement of games on a netball court.

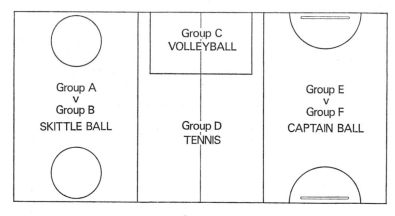

figure 2

1 *Skittle ball: enjoyment exercise and skill*

2 Variety and initiative: girls, too, can kick a ball

3 Equipment

As games storage baskets are likely to be used by a number of classes, the range of small apparatus contained in each basket should be as comprehensive as possible. It would be advantageous, where possible, to have one set of baskets for older juniors and another set for younger juniors and infants.

Not all the apparatus listed need be obtained for any one basket or set of baskets.

Equipment suitable for older juniors

Leather or moulded rubber footballs (size 4)

Medium and small plastic balls, including perforated balls

Leather, rubber or plastic rugby balls (size 4)

Small rubber balls

Rounders balls

Cricket balls (composition – junior size)

Quoits

Skittles (varying sizes)

Skipping ropes

Relay batons

Rounders and stoolball bats

Padder tennis bats and play bats

Junior hockey or shinty sticks

Small cricket bats or cricket bat shapes

Coloured braids

Equipment suitable for younger juniors and infants

Rubber or plastic inflated balls (size 3)

Rubber balls, 12·5 cm and 6·5 cm in diameter

Medium and small plastic balls, including perforated balls

Tennis balls, without covers

Quoits

Bean bags

Skittles (varying sizes)

Skipping ropes

Play bats and table tennis bats

Shinty sticks, cut down in length

Wooden cricket bat shapes

Coloured braids

In addition to the small apparatus contained in the baskets, a supply of other items of equipment will be required. Such equipment may include:

Long ropes
Canes of varying length
Assorted targets
Whistle
Playground chalk
Additional cricket apparatus, like pads, gloves and playground stumps
Rounders and stoolball posts
Netball posts
Highjump stands
Hoops.

The above lists appear formidable or even prohibitive, when thinking in terms of expenditure; however, in the primary school, it is often possible and wise to resort to improvised apparatus. In this way, not only is there a reduction in outlay, but, quite often, improvised apparatus is more suitable for the children who use it. It may be lighter and more easily carried than its original counterpart, and it may also occupy less space in storage cupboards, which are frequently inadequate for their purpose.

Reference has been made to cricket bat shapes. These can be purchased at approximately one-fifth of the price of junior cricket bats, but they can also be made. If a junior cricket bat is laid on a piece of stout plywood, its shape can be traced and cut from the wood, the rough edges should be smoothed, and the handle wrapped in adhesive tape so that there is protection against splinters. Play bats may also be improvised in this fashion, but, on the whole, these items are reasonably inexpensive.

Rounders bats may be quite costly and are certainly heavy for many primary school children, but lighter models may be cut from broom shanks. Relay batons may also be cut from broom shanks.

High jump stands are extremely useful and versatile pieces of equipment. Apart from being used for their original purpose, they can be used as net supports, uprights for hurdles, as targets and target supports. Unfortunately, they are rather costly, occupy a good deal of storage space because of their wide bases, and cannot easily be carried by small children. Again, improvisation can overcome the problems. The base can be made from a large empty jam or fruit tin, such as is thrown out by the school meals service. This is filled with cement, a hole pierced in the lid and the lid replaced and, if necessary, secured with adhesive tape. While the cement is still fluid, a bamboo cane is pushed through the hole and kept vertical while the cement sets. The cane can be made removable by wrapping a piece of paper round its base before it is thrust into the tin. When complete, the base may be painted in bright colours. A clothes peg of the spring–clip variety, attached to the upright, provides a shelf for the horizontal cane. The whole arrangement can then be stabilised quite adequately by the use of the group baskets. (See figure 3 and plate 5.)

The nets for use on this stand can be improvised by tying

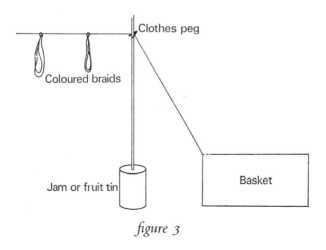

figure 3

coloured braids to a long rope: these braids are a particular boon to children with defective vision.

Assorted targets are a feature of games in the primary school. Targets can be painted or chalked on the playground itself or on walls. An example of a playground wall is illustrated in plate 6.

Hoops, skittles, playground stumps, rounder stands and highjump stands can all be utilised as targets. Benches, turned on their sides, make ideal goals for games of the soccer and hockey variety.

Stoolball posts each have a wooden, rectangular target attached to the top. However, stoolball is an adult game which is played with a bat, and players defend the target, which is at approximately shoulder height. For primary school children, this would mean defending a target well above shoulder height in nearly every case. Obviously, to restore the balance and so help the children to swing the bat correctly, the target must be lowered. The original target can be removed and replaced lower down the upright or a second target may be attached to the post. Perhaps the most convenient solution is a detachable target, made from plywood, hardboard or cardboard, fastened by drawing pins or long elastic bands, and which is therefore adjustable (figure 4). Similar adjustable targets may be attached to highjump stands or rounders posts.

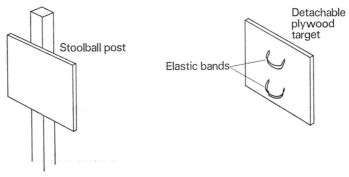

figure 4

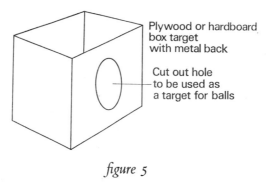

Plywood or hardboard
box target
with metal back

Cut out hole
to be used as
a target for balls

figure 5

Portable targets can be constructed, as in figure 5. The fronts and sides of these box targets are made in plywood or hardboard. If the back is made of metal, a successful shot or throw produces a most rewarding sound.

4 Schemes of work and the lesson plan

A certain amount of forward planning is advisable so that, as one games lesson follows another, there can be a build up of progressive skills and the opportunity for repetition and consolidation of those skills already acquired. However any scheme of work, subject as it is to vagaries of the weather, must, of necessity, be flexible.

It is impossible to forecast with any degree of accuracy what level of games performance may be expected from primary school children at any given age. As in gymnastics and dance, children of the same age group may display a wide range of aptitudes and ability. In spite of this, it is possible to make certain generalisations. Schemes of work for infants may be considered collectively: these schemes should offer activity which is largely imaginative and experimental. The children should have ample opportunity to manage their own body weight, to practise footwork and to move freely, while still being aware of their environment. They should also be encouraged to look for spaces, and there are many games which lend themselves to this. Games of the tag variety have much to recommend them, as they combine the above features with another important feature of infant work, namely excitement. Without an element of excitement to capture their interest, children's attention soon begins to wander. In younger children, this occurs quite soon, and, when it happens, there is a greater risk of minor accidents taking place and the lesson becomes unsatisfactory from an educational standpoint.

Apparatus selected for infants should be light and easy to handle. The children will take more care of it if it is brightly coloured and visually attractive. Individual practices are to be encouraged: at this age, generally speaking, the challenge offered by the apparatus is sufficient in itself and competition between individuals or groups is not desirable. On the other hand, the children soon begin to enjoy partner work in which apparatus is shared, and this is valuable early training in the important social aspect of games, which should not be neglected.

The coaching of set skills, in other words those skills taught in relation to major or national games, is both unnecessary and unsatisfactory for this age group. Infants tend to learn more quickly and more readily by discovering the variety of things they can do with small apparatus.

In planning a scheme of work for infants, the teacher should remember that these younger children soon become bored with activities requiring a good deal of concentrated prolonged attention. For this reason, there must be frequent changes of both activity and apparatus, and the whole games period should not last for more than about twenty minutes.

Below is a summary of the features, which should be considered in the preparation of a scheme of work for infant games.

1 Activity should be imaginative and experimental.
2 Apparatus should be easy to handle.
3 There should be a wide variety of apparatus available.
4 Individual activities are to be encouraged.
5 Partner activities are suitable, if shared and not competitive.
6 Social activities are desirable.
7 Learning comes through discovery.
8 Frequent changes of activities and apparatus are essential.
9 Lessons should be brief.

In relation to the basic aims of games in the primary school, it seems reasonable to suggest that, for infants, greater emphasis should be placed on enjoyment than on exercise and the acquisition of skill. If enjoyment is present, one can rest assured that exercise and skill will emerge.

As children get older, the teacher should offer opportunities for extending the range of skills practised. The children should still be encouraged to discover how apparatus can be used, but now they should be weaned from mere experimentation and taught to analyse their work. Activities and ways of improving these activities should be discussed by the teacher and the children, and the members of the class should be encouraged to watch each other at practice since observation is a vital part of learning.

As skills are practised and improved upon, they should then be combined and used to supplement each other. For instance, infants start by playing with bean bags, throwing them quite freely: later, they may throw and catch them. As familiarity with the apparatus decreases the difficulty of the activity, a ball can be substituted for the bean bag. As the children get older and their ability increases, throwing and catching techniques should be analysed and practised. Skill is acquired or improved as the thrower aims at a target, painted on a wall; the rebound makes a greater demand upon the catcher, who may be either the thrower or a partner to the thrower. When a batter or striker is placed between the thrower and the target, the skills involved become even more difficult, varied and numerous.

Competition should be introduced as soon as the children have sufficient skill to enable them to enjoy a competitive situation; some children may reach this stage before others.

Initially, competition should be between one child and another or between one child and two others. By this time, the child has acquired an awareness of his environment, the apparatus and other players in relationship to him. This is, in fact, the competitive situation which exists in most team games. At any given moment, the player with the ball should be aware of a partner who is to receive the ball, and of the opposing player who will endeavour to prevent or intercept this exchange. Each member of the trio has his or her own function in relation to the other two players. Although the composition of this trio is constantly changing throughout a game, there is, nevertheless, this ever present relationship between three players.

The two versus one situation is sometimes referred to as an overload practice. This is illustrated by plate 7, where two boys combine in an attempt to defeat the goalkeeper.

A scheme of work for older children should incorporate the following features.

1 The opportunity to acquire skill.
2 The opportunity to consolidate this skill.
3 The opportunity to improve skill by observation and analysis.
4 Partner and group work.
5 Competition, when children are ready for this.
6 Small-side team games, incorporating earlier skill practices.

Finally, any scheme of work must be adjusted to the seasons. On cold winter mornings, all activities should be vigorous and games periods held outdoors should be brief. On the other hand, hot summer days encourage the practice of more leisurely skills with ample time for question and answer coaching techniques.

The *lesson plan* provides a means of implementing the proposals in the scheme of work, in logical sequence and within the framework of one lesson. The following plan suggests a way of organising the games period so that the optimum acquisition and coaching of skills can be balanced with the practice and exploitation of these skills in an active enjoyable way.

1 Introduction.
2 Class activity.
3 Games and athletics.

1 Introduction

In this part of the lesson, the children are encouraged to experiment individually, with their own choice of apparatus, and also to practise skills already known to them.

As soon as the baskets have been placed around the playing area and have been checked by the group leaders, the children should be permitted to select any piece of apparatus from their own baskets. They then use this to experiment or practise freely. In order to overcome the problem of one child selecting the same piece of apparatus every time, the children are asked, after a very short interval, to change their apparatus for something different.

This introduction only lasts for two or three minutes, but it serves to warm up the class and enables the teacher to organise the distribution of any additional apparatus he intends to use during the lesson.

2 Class Activity

This is an extremely important part of the lesson in which children use the same apparatus, while receiving general and individual coaching or stimulation from the teacher.

Shortage of apparatus may create a problem at this stage. For instance, it is very unlikely that every child in the class can be supplied with a football. However, two class or group activities may be conducted at the same time. While girls are working on tennis, using play bats and small balls, boys may be undergoing coaching in soccer, using large balls. On the other hand, one piece of apparatus may be shared by two or more pupils. For example, only one ball is required between two pupils when simple passing skills are being coached.

Various coaching techniques may be employed in this part of the lesson and some of these methods are discussed below.

(a) **Demonstration** Demonstrations of games skills can be given by the teacher or by children selected by the teacher. The latter situation is usually more productive as the children gain prestige from participating in demonstrations and respond to this encouragement; moreover, children are often more ready to imitate each other than to imitate the teacher. However, if no pupil is capable of interpreting the teacher's requirements, the latter may have to resort to a personal demonstration.

Demonstrations, particularly those required of children, should always be observed critically, but the criticism should be positive. Children who are practising skills incorrectly should never be singled out for demonstration in order to discuss their faults. If an activity is not demonstrated to the teacher's satisfaction, the latter should find some part of the activity which calls for a word of praise and, having offered this, invite the performers, together with the other children, to suggest alternative ways of improving the activity.

Any demonstration must be followed up by the opportunity for practice.

(b) Experimentation   With this technique, pupils are invited to attempt as many different ways of practising a movement or technique as they can discover. They are then encouraged to select by trial and error the most successful method of practising. Of course, the wise teacher will unobtrusively influence this selection by stimulating the right kind of individual analysis. This analysis may become a little clearer in the light of the following paragraph.

(c) Question and answer   This is a simple but effective method of analysis, involving a good deal of class participation. The questions put by the teacher should demand thought by the pupils and, wherever possible, a single word reply should be discouraged. Suitable replies should be based on either the experience or the observation of the children. Answers based on conjecture are only satisfactory if these answers can be tested by the children in a practical way.

The most satisfactory coaching systems usually include a combination of the above techniques, as illustrated in the following example. The teacher asks John to demonstrate the catching of a cricket ball. In order to ensure that the ball reaches John accurately and at a suitable speed, the teacher is careful in his selection of the thrower; alternatively, he can carry out this task himself. After one or two successful catches, the teacher asks, 'What did John do, when his fingers touched the ball?' As a result of their observation, the children may well answer, 'He drew the ball towards him'. They are then instructed, 'Watch again. How did he hold his hands?' Again, after an acceptable reply, the teacher may ask, 'Why do you think he placed his hands together?'

In order to get the full benefit of the question and answer technique, it is necessary to supplement the theory with practice. A number of coaching hints for various class activities are given in chapter 5, which deals specifically with the coaching and practice of skills.

The scheme of work for older primary school children should cater for the coaching and execution of skills in a competitive situation. The coaching aspect of competitive skills takes place mainly in the class activity part of the lesson. As already suggested, competition may be between one player and another, as in the coaching of tennis, or between one player and two others, as in the coaching of soccer, hockey and netball. Here is an example of how the class activity part of a lesson might be conducted.

The girls are arranged in pairs with a play bat each and one small rubber ball per pair. A tennis net is painted or chalked, as the target, on a playground wall. In their pairs, the girls play the ball alternately, aiming to bounce the ball just above the target line. This rebound practice enables the teacher to coach such features as keeping the face of the bat 'open', that is, at right-angles to the direction of the swing, correct back-swing with follow through and good positioning of the feet.

In the meantime, after passing practice in pairs the boys are given a large ball between three players so that two may endeavour to achieve consecutive passes along the ground, while the third player attempts to intercept. The boys should change roles frequently, so either an interception or six successful passes should be set as the point at which this should take place. Aspects of coaching might feature playing the ball with either foot, seeking or creating spaces and moving to the ball.

The class activity may occupy some five to ten minutes of a thirty-minute games period. However, the actual time to be spent on this section of the lesson should not be rigidly predetermined. It should be influenced by the requirements of the pupils and by the degree of success enjoyed during this part of the lesson.

3 Games and Athletics

The terms 'games' and 'athletics' have been used as a collective heading for those activities which are competitive and provide opportunities for scoring in one form or another. Competition may take place between teams or between individuals; or, on the other hand, it may well occur when an individual attempts to better his or her own previous best performance – as is found very frequently in athletics. Competition may be against a clock, a height or a distance.

Natural ability should be allied to skills previously acquired or recently gained and practised in the earlier part of the lesson, and coaching should be incidental and interfere as little as possible with the participation and enjoyment of the game.

Small-side team games, tend to lead a high scoring frequency, are recommended. The claim that 'success breeds success' is particularly true of games in the primary school. Children should not only be given every opportunity to score goals, points or runs, but these successes should be recognised and recorded. The teacher should never terminate a game without asking for the result and the score. Even in individual events, like certain athletics activities, the children should be encouraged to record their scores so that these may be compared with their totals recorded in earlier lessons.

Games of the 'sudden death' variety should be avoided at all costs. If in a bat and ball game a child is out to the very first ball, without the chance of an early return to batting, that child is bound to feel discouraged or frustrated. The child gains neither enjoyment nor exercise and certainly has little opportunity to acquire skill. Alternatively, if all players are allowed six successful strikes, the more able players will gain high scores, while even the least able will enjoy some measure of success. However, those in opposition to the strikers are also entitled to their reward, by dismissing the strikers. The best of both worlds is obtained by playing 'non-stop' games which produce a rapid turnover of scores and dismissals. Non-stop cricket is a superb example of this kind of game in that the children may bowl, field and bat five or six times in the course of a ten-minute session.

All games should be active, with a minimum of time being wasted. Good preparation means that explanations can be brief and confined to the basic essentials required in order to get the games started. Games of the warm-up variety, particularly those not requiring apparatus, e.g., tag or dodge and mark, may also be utilised in the introductory part of the lesson.

Details of all the games mentioned above, and of many other games suitable for primary school children, are to be found in chapter 6.

The actual selection of games to be played will be determined to some extent by the apparatus available, the area and surface to be used, the age of the children concerned and the weather. However, the main consideration must always be the requirements of the children, based upon the teacher's observation of them.

The lesson should be concluded by the apparatus being returned to the baskets and the contents of the baskets being checked by the group leaders. While this checking takes place, the remaining children may be employed in activities which do not require apparatus. Finally, the baskets and all additional items of equipment are returned to the games store.

5 The coaching and practice of skills

It cannot be overemphasised that, in order to play and enjoy most games, children in the primary school should be encouraged to practise and become familiar with apparatus. This is achieved, initially, through experimentation, and then by repetition of acquired movements or skills: these skills may be acquired by discovery or by imitation. The discovery approach has particular merit for children of the infant school and for juniors in the lower age group.

For the very young, the lesson plan should to some extent be modified, as games are incorporated in the infant activity period and cannot, in themselves, be regarded as a lesson. Team games are generally not very suitable, as simplicity must be the keynote. Consequently, the activities should be orientated towards the individual, while abundant coaching and encouragement are offered. For this reason it is neither practical nor desirable to distinguish between class activities and actual games.

In teaching infants, emphasis should be placed on inspiring a desire to experiment with small apparatus. There should be a very wide range available, and the child should be given, where possible, complete freedom to choose which apparatus to use and to select the activity to be practised.

Reception classes – 5 to 6 years old

In these early months, the wide range of apparatus available, the unlimited variety of activities possible, and the unpredictable movement of a large, soft ball, form an adequate challenge to the children and afford them ample opportunities for the acquisition of skill. At this stage, the teacher is probably fully occupied in obtaining complete class participation and in endeavouring to stimulate the more reluctant children into taking the plunge. In dealing with these problems, the teacher will probably find that exciting activities of the tag or chase variety and games of the party type can be of great assistance.

Activities which fall into this category are listed below and will be described in detail in chapter 6.

Crusts and crumbs	It
Scoring runs	Do this, do that
Filling the basket	Ships, lifeboats and aeroplanes
Fishes in the net	Catch your partner's tail
Follow my leader	Do as I do

Older infants and juniors in the lower age range

As individual skill develops through experimentation, the teacher begins to impose limitations on free activity; this is sometimes known as an 'indirect teaching approach'. As in educational gymnastics, children are set certain tasks. These tasks are subject to interpretation in a number of ways and still allow a certain amount of experimentation. Although these tasks are not necessarily related to actual games, they do require the children to perform functional skills of one kind or another.

Below are examples of tasks and questions which might be put to a class employed in activities with balls.

Can you roll the ball along the ground, chase it and stop it?
Can you roll the ball at different speeds?
How many ways, or directions, can you roll the ball?
How many different body parts can you use to roll the ball?
Can you roll the ball with one part of the body and stop it with a different part?
Show me how you can make the ball bounce.
Can you bounce it high? Low? Medium height?
Can you bounce the ball in different ways and catch it?
How many parts of the body can you use to bounce the ball?

TIGERS
3 FOOTBALLS
4 RUBBER QUOITS
6 SMALL BALLS
6 ROPES
3 HOCKEY STICKS
1 SKITTLE
1 RUGBY BALL
6 PLAYBATS
   BRAIDS

3 The basket

4 *The area: six groups on a netball court*

Can you throw the ball in the air and catch it?

Can you do this again, but let the ball bounce before you catch it?

Can you move while bouncing the ball?

Can you move while throwing the ball and catching it?

Can you throw the ball at a wall and catch it as it comes back?

Can you jump in the air and bounce the ball?

With 'vertical streaming' and 'family grouping' in the infant school, the activity period may allow complete freedom to experiment for some children, while indirect teaching is being offered to others.

A skill may be practised for its own sake and for the enjoyment it provides, rather than always being regarded as a step towards the playing of a major or national game. However, there are few physical skills practised with apparatus on playground or field which are not in some way related to games or athletics. For this reason, the following simplified coaching hints are classified according to their function in the playing of games. It should be appreciated that many of the following skills could well meet the requirements of more than one classification.

1 Ball-handling

(a) Skills employed in games of the netball/basketball type Balls used should range in size from 13 cm diameter balls to size 5 netballs. Plastic inflated balls are lighter and cheaper than leather balls. Rubber balls are useful, but inflated, moulded rubber balls are particularly suitable because they have excellent handling surfaces and retain their initial weight under wet conditions.

1 PASSING The first consideration should be accuracy. The children should pass the ball in a straight line to a partner's chest or stomach. Passes should be practised, using first two hands and then one hand. Alternatives are bounce passes and overhead passes: the latter should again be as straight as

C

possible, even if the thrower has to jump from the ground in order to achieve it.

2 CATCHING OR RECEIVING Pupils are taught to move towards the ball, getting their bodies behind it. Two hands are used for catching. Arms and fingers are extended towards the ball and, on contact, the ball is drawn into the body.

3 BOUNCING AND DRIBBLING Either hand may be used and the children should be encouraged to bounce the ball to front, rear, either side and even around the body. The fingers are used to stroke the ball downwards, controlling the height of the bounce at about waist level or a little below. The player's knees should be bent and the feet spaced comfortably, and the free arm should act as an aid to balance. Bouncing practices can be executed on the spot, around the body, as described, or on the move: this last may involve manoeuvres around and between skittles or similar obstacles.

4 SHOOTING The ball is held in two hands, with the shooting hand on top. The lower hand steadies the ball, while the body and shooting arm extend. The completed projection may be executed with the feet on the ground or with the player actually in flight.

Class activities employing the above techniques:
> Throwing, two handed, at large wall targets
> Passing in pairs from standing positions, gradually increasing the distance between the players
> Passing in pairs on the move
> Dribbling around the body and in open spaces
> Dribbling around skittles and hoops
> Dribbling and passing in pairs
> Competitive passing with emphasis on using space. This requires groups of three players and is sometimes known as pig in the middle.

Games involving netball/basketball skills include:
> Dodge and mark

Wandering ball
Dodge ball – individual or team
Defending the post or skittle
Dribbling and passing relays, using skittles or hoops
Handball
Skittle ball
Captain ball
Netball (possibly modified)

(b) Games of the volleyball/Newcombe type Balls used should be of the plastic, inflatable type, and it is recommended that their dimensions should not exceed those of a size 3 football. If leather balls are used, they should not be fully inflated and must be of the laceless variety.

1   PLAYING THE BALL HIGH   Children are taught to push the ball into the air, above head height. The palms of both hands face the ball and the fingers are used to push it, controlling the upward direction.

2   PLAYING THE BALL LOW   The fists are clenched and the heels of both hands are placed together. The ball is played with the insides of the wrists or lower forearms.

3   SERVING   The ball is released by the non-striking hand and played underhand by the striking hand. The fingers of the latter are clenched and the area striking the ball is the front of the fist and the inside of the wrist. A good follow-through action is desirable in order to control direction and reduce the impact required to give the ball distance.

4   SPIKING   The player uses the fingers of one hand, as in playing the ball high. However, he jumps high into the air, in order to exert downward pressure on the ball. As he jumps, the body is twisted through a semicircle. This means that a ball, pushed forward by a player at the rear of the court, may be spiked over a net in the same forward direction by another player of the same team.

Class activities employing the above techniques:

Playing the ball high and low, individually

Repeat in pairs, playing the ball to each other

Serving the ball above a net chalked or painted on a wall

Playing the ball to a partner over a net, which is a little above head height

In threes, one playing the ball to a spiker, who stands between the other two players. The spiker, in turn, plays the ball downwards to the third player, who catches the ball and then reverses the process

Games associated with the above activities are simplified or modified versions of volleyball itself, including Newcombe. Early games should permit players to throw the ball across the net and to catch the ball before returning it. Later games may require the participants to play the ball, as described above, after catching it. Still later, the catching is omitted, although the children are allowed to play the ball more than once consecutively. This leads on to games which permit the ball to be played only once by each player before it is returned across the net.

The games may start with only one or two players per side, but may eventually develop into a game of volleyball with six players in each team.

(c) Throwing small balls, as in cricket, rounders and athletic activities Balls used may be composition cricket balls, rounders balls, rubber balls, tennis balls or perforated plastic balls. Plastic balls are less satisfactory for older juniors, but they are safer in the vicinity of windows. Bean bags can be used by younger children.

The thrower should adopt a sideways stance with the non-throwing arm pointing roughly in the direction of the throw. Whether the throw is underhand or overhand, there should be adequate backswing and follow through. This aids both accuracy and distance. The ball should be held in the fingers and not in the palm of the hand. When trying for distance, the thrower must initiate the movement from his or her feet. Rotation is taken up by the hips and then the shoulders, so that the arm comes through last with the elbow under the wrist, in a whiplike action. The rotation is continued after the ball has been released. This action may be observed in a javelin thrower.

Bowling for cricket is practised in a similar way, but as the bowling arm follows through it is kept straight and, to all intents and purposes, moves through a vertical plane. The ball is released immediately after it has passed its highest point.

Class activities employing the above techniques:

Throwing the ball at wall targets or mounted targets

Throwing the ball to a partner

Throwing the ball to a wicketkeeper, who catches above a skittle or playground stumps

The ball can be thrown by a group of players, circling a target. If the target is a slip catching cradle or a metal dustbin lid, with a fluted surface, the ball will rebound at different angles. This adds catching practice to throwing practice

Throwing bean bags at skittles or targets (younger children only)

Bowling at large skittles, playground stumps or stumps marked on walls

Games associated with the above activities include:

Non-stop cricket

Rounders

Stoolball

Modified baseball or softball

(d) Handling a rugby ball Balls used may be of the inflated plastic or soft rubber type; leather or moulded rubber balls are suitable, but are heavier and more expensive. Moulded rubber balls are very good to handle and retain their initial weight under wet conditions.

1   PASSING   Here, the main consideration is accuracy. The ball is passed, so far as distance permits, in a horizontal straight line to the receiver's stomach. If passing is executed while the receiver is on the move, the ball is aimed a little in front of the stomach, enabling him to run onto the pass.

The thrower holds the ball in his fingers with the palms facing each other. The fingers themselves are extended towards the pointed end of the ball. There is a slight backswing before the ball is moved across the body to be passed sideways and slightly backwards. It is released when the arms are extended.

When passing on the run to a partner on the left, the ball is moved to the right as the left foot comes forward, and released as the right foot comes forward: this produces a vital turn of the hips as the pass is made and the thrower turns to face the receiver.

2   CATCHING OR RECEIVING A PASS   The players should run onto a pass, take the ball in two hands and pull it into the body. The ball is quickly adjusted in the hands and carried in the passing position described above.

3   CATCHING A HIGH BALL FROM THE FRONT   The players are encouraged from the outset to keep their eyes on the ball. They must move to the ball, forming a catching cradle with the arms and hands. For added security, the elbows are tucked into the body.

Class activities employing the above techniques:

Passing in pairs, threes or fours
Repeat, walking, trotting and, then, running
Individual passing at wall targets
Group circle passing, with players facing outwards
Running, zigzag fashion between obstacles, carrying a ball in the passing position
Two against one passing activities

Repeat with two against three or three against four as an overload practice

In pairs, one throws the ball high so that his partner may practise the cradle catch

Games associated with the above activities include:

Zigzag relays in which participants carry and pass a rugby ball

Handball, using a rugby ball

Murder ball (to be played only on a soft grass pitch)

Wandering ball

Touch rugby

Gainings, played by throwing a rugby ball

Number call: one player throws a rugby ball high into the air and calls the number of one of his group. The player called endeavours to cradle catch the ball. Points are awarded for successful catches.

2 Ball-striking or -kicking

(a) **Games of the tennis type** Apparatus used may range from junior tennis racquets to table tennis bats. It may include badminton racquets, squash racquets, padder tennis bats, batinton equipment, and a whole range of play bats, including home-made ones. Balls used may be selected from tennis balls, preferably with well-worn covers for younger children, small rubber balls and perforated plastic balls.

For convenience, it is assumed in the following sequences that the players are right-handed. Obviously, for left-handed players, the positions will be reversed.

I   THE STANCE   The racquet or bat is held comfortably in the right hand as if the player were about to chop wood with the edge of it, and it is then held comfortably across the front of the body. If the implement is a racquet, then it is usual to support the throat in the left hand: the throat is the junction of the handle's shaft with the racquet head. As he faces his opponent, the player spreads his feet a little, leans his weight slightly forward onto the balls of his feet and keeps his knees slightly bent.

2   THE FOREHAND STROKE   As the ball approaches, the player moves his left foot across the front of his body so that he turns through almost 180 degrees and presents his left shoulder to his opponent. Keeping his eyes on the ball, he swings his racquet or bat backwards in a wide, horizontal arc between the levels of the shoulder and waist. The racquet head or bat is then swung at the ball in a horizontal plane with a follow through action. On impact with the ball the face of the racquet or bat should be 'open', i.e., the face of the racquet or bat is both vertical and at right-angles to the direction of the stroke.

3   THE BACKHAND STROKE   The handle is rotated slightly in the hand to maintain an open face as the racquet or bat is swung at the ball. A little experimentation will soon establish the correct backhand grip.

The right foot is then moved across the front of the body as the left foot was in the forehand movement. The right shoulder is presented to the opponent as a backswing is executed. From this stage the same principles should be observed as for the forehand stroke.

4   SERVING OVERHEAD   The player should assume a left-foot forward stance with the ball held in the left hand. He throws the ball about 60 cm above head height so that, were it allowed to complete its fall, it would hit the ground about 30 cm ahead of his left foot and a few centimetres to the right of it. Obviously, there will be many deviations from this pattern in view of differing styles and physical dimensions, and it is therefore stressed that the above measurements are merely generalisations based on average beginners in primary schools. The racquet is swung through a vertical arc and meets the ball just after the racquet head has passed through its highest point.

This service is quite difficult for all but a few older primary school children.

5   UNDERHAND SERVICES The ball is held in the left hand at arm's length and at shoulder height. It is released as the bat or racquet is swung forward in a vertical plane to make contact with the ball just below waist height.

For badminton, the underhand service is always used. It is recommended that the cheaper, outdoor shuttles be used for badminton practices as these tend to be slower in flight and, in any case, are much more satisfactory for outdoor use. The general principles applied to tennis strokes apply also to badminton strokes, except that more wrist action is used in badminton.

The game of batinton is strongly recommended for older juniors. Batinton bats may also be used in conjunction with outdoor shuttlecocks. The bats combine the whiplike shaft of the badminton racquet with the solid face of a play bat. The heavier face imparts greater impetus to the shuttle, therefore helping the children to achieve distance in their stroke play.

Class activities employing the above techniques:

    Individual practice of bouncing a ball on a bat or racquet
    Individual practice of bouncing a ball on the ground using a bat or a racquet
    Rebound practice against a wall, using bat and ball (a painted or chalked tennis net is helpful here)
    Playing the ball to a partner
    Repeat over a net or a cane, resting on skittles or other supports
    With a partner, alternate rebound practice, using a wall net
    With a partner, throwing and catching a rubber quoit across a net

Games associated with the above activities include:

    Quoit tennis
    Rebound tennis
    Padder tennis

Batinton

Badminton, with modified rules and use of an outdoor shuttlecock

Pat ball or modified fives

Hand tennis, played with a beach ball

(b) Games of the rounders and stoolball type

1   FIELDING, BOWLING AND PITCHING   The skills of throwing and catching a small ball have already been described. In fielding, one of the basic fundamentals is moving quickly to the ball, and this cannot be overstressed.

2   STRIKING   Children should adopt a sideways stance, with the feet comfortably apart, so that the left shoulder points directly to the pitcher or bowler, assuming that the striker is right-handed. There should be adequate backswing in a horizontal plane, approximating to shoulder level. The striker should always follow through to gain distance and increase accuracy.

Class activities employing the above techniques:

Individual practice of throwing at shoulder high wall targets

Throwing at posts or targets mounted on posts

Repeat the above, with a striker defending the target

In threes, pitching, striking and fielding practice

In fours, as above, but with backstop practice

Picking up and throwing at a target or to a partner while on the run

Games associated with the above activities:

Rounders

Stoolball

Modified versions of baseball or its Canadian counterpart, softball

Tip and run (similar to non-stop cricket)

Wild ball, using rounders or play bats to propel the ball

Hot rice

(c) Soccer type games

1   KICKING   (i) The low drive or shooting technique. The non-kicking foot is placed alongside the ball. The head is kept over the ball as the instep of the kicking foot meets the ball and follows through. The toe is extended and kept well down.

(ii) Passing. This is mainly executed with the inside of the foot, unless distance is required, in which case the drive or lob is employed. The outside of the foot may be used occasionally to produce a short sideways pass.

(iii) The lob or lifted ball. The kicker places his non-kicking foot slightly to the rear of the ball and leans backward as the kick is executed. The instep meets the ball and the follow-through action is rather across the body. For this reason, the run up to the ball is at an angle to the eventual path taken by the ball.

(iv) The punt. This kick is used by goalkeepers when attempting to achieve height and distance. The ball is held by two hands at arm's length and dropped onto the instep of the kicking foot. The latter is swung high in a follow-through action.

2   TRAPPING   This practice is employed by players to stop the ball from bouncing or rolling away from their immediate control. As a ball approaches along the ground, the player extends the appropriate foot towards it and withdraws this foot gradually, thus slowing down the ball on arrival. A bouncing ball may be trapped by the sole of the foot, the inside or outside of the foot, or by the chest. In every case, the player's head and body weight are moved over the ball as the ball comes to the ground. When receiving any ball, it is essential for the player to move towards it.

3   HEADING   The forehead is used for this. The muscles of the neck are flexed to give impetus and direction to the ball. Again, the player must move to the ball, even if it means getting off the ground to do so, and he must keep his eyes on the ball as long as it is physically possible to do so.

4   THE THROW IN   Both hands are placed on the ball, with the palms facing each other. Both feet must be kept on the ground while the ball is thrown directly over the head in a forward direction. There must be no twist of the body during the throw.

5   DRIBBLING   The insides and outsides of both feet are used. The head is kept well over the ball, which should be kept in close proximity to the player's feet. Children should watch the ball, but also be aware of their surroundings by constantly glancing about them. For this reason, dribbling should be practised frequently, once the basic skill has been acquired, among other people or obstacles.

Class activities employing the above techniques:

    Individual practices of dribbling and juggling the ball with
        the feet, knees and head
    Kicking at targets or against a wall
    In pairs, passing and receiving
    Repeat the above, on the move
    Two against one (pig in the middle)
    Consecutive heading, individually
    Consecutive heading in pairs or groups
    Dribbling round a circle (e.g., the centre circle of a soccer
        pitch) with change of direction on a whistle blast

Games associated with the above activities:

    Soccer or heading tennis
    Five or six a side soccer
    Crab football
    Skittle ball, played with the feet
    Defending the post or central pillar ball, played with the feet
    Wandering ball, played with the feet
    Dribbling and passing relays

(d) Kicking a rugby ball

1   THE PUNT   The ball is held at arm's length in two hands and dropped onto the instep of the kicking foot. The latter is

swung high in a follow-through action. This is similar to a goalkeeper's punt in soccer.

2   DROP KICK   The technique is similar to that of the punt, but the ball is dropped to the ground on its pointed end. It is kicked as it touches the ground.

3   PLACE KICK   If height is required, the ball is set on its point, with its long axis leaning slightly towards the kicker. If distance is required, the long axis is inclined in the direction the ball is expected to take. In both cases, the toe of the kicking foot is used and there is a pronounced follow-through action.

4   DRIBBLING   This is executed by the feet and shins of both legs. The head is kept over the ball, the arms are used to assist balance and the ball is kept as close to the feet as possible.

Class activities employing the above techniques:

Individual dribbling
Gainings, played on a field
Place kicks and punts to a partner
Repeat to drop the ball into marked circles on a field

Games associated with the above activities are usually also concerned with the handling of a ball. Consequently, the games are listed under that heading. However, some of the class activities, like gainings, can be practised, using a points scoring system to add interest.

(e) Hockey/shinty type games   The stick is held with the left hand above the right, and the hands are spaced so that the player does not need to bend unduly when playing the ball. However, it is important that children learn to keep their hands well up the stick at an early stage: the habit of spacing the hands too widely is difficult to break, and it is often formed as a result of sticks being too long and too heavy.

The children should be taught to push the ball, keeping it close to the stick.

In striking a ball for shooting or passing, they should be encouraged to keep the stick low, both in the backswing and the follow-through.

Class activities employing the above techniques:

Hitting the ball and then running after it

Repeat, catching up with the ball and hitting it a second or third time

Dribble the ball round a skittle, with particular emphasis on moving round to the right

Roll the ball away, chase it, stop it with a stick and dribble it back.

Rebound hitting against a wall or against a bench turned on its side

Passing to a stationary partner and then to a moving partner

Continuous passing to two or more partners, changing the angle of passing

Two against one (pig in the middle)

Games associated with the above activities:

Modified versions of hockey or shinty

Skittle ball, using hockey or shinty sticks

Defending the post, with hockey or shinty sticks

Wandering ball

Dribbling and passing relays

(f) Batting – cricket type games The right-handed batsman holds the bat as though he were about to chop wood with its edge, ensuring that the left hand is nearer the upper end of the handle. He adopts a comfortable sideways stance, with his left shoulder towards the bowler, and rests the bottom edge of the bat on the ground, behind his right toe. The head is turned so that both eyes can see an approaching ball clearly.

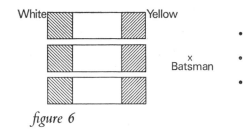

figure 6

The batsman should be taught to move his feet to the ball and swing his bat in a vertical arc down the line of the ball. Backswing should be pronounced.

He goes forward to meet balls pitched close to the bat in order to hit them at a low point in their bounce. This is impossible for balls pitched well short of the bat. In this situation, he moves back to hit the ball as it falls low, having passed the highest point of its bounce.

Class activities employing the above techniques:

Individual practice of throwing up a ball and driving it with a bat at a target or between skittles

Batting practice with one partner bowling

Plate 6 and figure 6 illustrate how the batsman can be given variety in the 'length' of the ball and the angle at which his stroke must be played in relation to the line of the ball's approach. The rectangles are marked in different coloured chalk on the playground. The bowler stands about 4 metres from the batsman and lobs the ball at the rectangle of his choice. A ball which bounces on the yellow mark, nearer to the bat is a well pitched-up ball, requiring the batsman to play forward. A ball landing on the white mark further from the bat, is a short-pitched ball, and the batsman should play back.

Additional partners may fulfil other cricket functions like keeping wicket and fielding.

Games associated with the above activities:

Non-stop cricket

39

Hot rice

Defending the post. In this version of the game, the post is represented by a skittle or a single cricket stump erected on a grass area. The batsman defends the post with a cricket bat or bat shape

3 Athletics

(a) Running

1   SPRINTING   The knees should be well picked up. The body leans forward without any bend at the hips. The children must be taught to run through the finishing mark without slowing down.

2   STARTING   The front foot toes the line and the rear leg is bent. The latter is straightened to drive the runner forward. This drive is accompanied by a punching action of bent arms.

3   RELAY BATON CHANGING   This is achieved while both runners are moving at speed. The baton is given by the left hand and received by the right. On receipt, the next runner transfers the baton immediately to his left hand.

4   HURDLING   Pupils must be encouraged to *run* over the hurdles, instead of jumping over them. There should be no perceptible change of stride in hurdling and the same leg should lead in every clearance.

(b) Jumping

1   LONG JUMP   The performer should hit the take-off board at maximum speed. A punching action of the arms assists take-off. The upper part of the body is kept vertical in the air. Both feet are brought forward just before landing and the body should fall forward as it lands.

2   HIGH JUMP   No particular method needs to be sought in the primary school. A short, springy run-up is required and the body leans back on take-off. The non-driving leg is swung upwards to assist lift and to add force to the driving leg

5 *Improvisation: baskets with high jump stand*

6 *The playground wall: cricket skills*

7 *Overload practices: two versus one*

through reaction. The hips are raised to bring the body as near to the horizontal as possible.

(c) Throwing Throwing techniques in the primary school are associated with throwing a ball or a rubber quoit.

Class activities employing the above techniques will obviously consist of those events listed above, together with group practices of baton changing.

Games associated with the above involve competitions in the various events.

For high jumps and long jumps, including standing broad jump, a points scoring system might be substituted for actual heights and distances.

Plate 9 and figure 7 illustrate a suggested grid marking for standing broad jump. Points are indicated at each interval. The

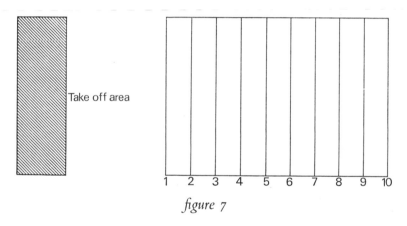

figure 7

least able performer should be capable of scoring at least one point in his jump. However, the top mark of ten points should be just beyond the reach of the most able performer. Consequently, the good jumpers are extended in trying to reach distant marks and the poorer performers are encouraged by the way their combined points totals increase with each jump.

Points intervals can be similarly marked on adhesive tape which can be attached to the sides of high jump stands.

Aggregate competitions are popular in athletics and give lots of scope for the all-round performer. Points scored by throwing are added to points scored for running and for jumping; these points may be acquired by individuals or by small teams, pooling their individual talents.

6 Games and athletics

The third and longest section of the primary school games period should be devoted to the actual playing of games or to participation in athletics activities.

Various national and international governing bodies of sport have devised rules and instructions which deal with competition in games and athletics, but we do not intend to reproduce them in this book. The primary school teacher responsible for teaching games is obviously more concerned with those activities which meet the requirements of the children. While some of these requirements may be satisfied by simplified or modified versions of officially recognised games, many other games, which have no recorded or recognisable origins, may be even more suitable. Indeed, some may have been devised by children themselves.

The games suggested in this chapter are offered because of their particular suitability for primary school children. They provide ample scope for them to obtain enjoyment and exercise, and to practise those skills which sound teaching has enabled them to acquire. Many of the games listed may be known by different names in different areas. Certain names may be associated in the minds of some teachers with games differing from those listed. This is inevitable since a good number of the activities have their origins in children's play, both in and out of school, acquiring names which the players thought appropriate.

Rules are reduced to an absolute minimum. Additional rules may be introduced as the need arises. Often, the most satisfactory rules are those devised by the children themselves, under the guidance of the teacher. The rules should make a game simple to play, and in the most interesting way. If rules reduce enjoyment and participation, they should be discarded.

In the following games the bare framework of instructions

and rules is presented in order that children can begin playing quickly and easily. As suggested above, further rules and playing requirements, or limitations, are the province of both teacher and children.

For ease of reference, the games are grouped, as far as possible, according to their main skill function.

Infant Games

What time is it, Mr Wolf? Mr Wolf is often initially played by the teacher, who walks slowly forward, followed at a short distance by the children. The children call in unison, 'What time is it, Mr Wolf?' To which the wolf answers, 'Two o'clock' or 'Five o'clock'. After a number of calls, the wolf eventually replies, 'Dinner time', and turns about to catch the children, who will run away and try to get to the safe area. Children once caught become Wolf cubs and assist Mr Wolf.

It (or he) Two or three children are designated 'it', and given coloured braids to wear. They try to catch other children. Those who are caught change places with their captors.

Tag This is another version of 'it'. However, in tag, the chaser is merely required to touch his prey.

Crusts and crumbs A class is divided into two lines facing each other near the middle of the play area. One end of the area is designated 'crusts' and the other 'crumbs'. When the teacher calls, 'crusts', the team nearer to that end runs to it for safety. The opposing team tries to catch these runners before they reach safety. Players who are caught must join the opposition. However, when the teacher calls 'crumbs' the situation is reversed. Excitement tends to be increased if the teacher lingers on the first part of each word.

Scoring runs This is a competition in running, hopping or skipping. On a given signal from the teacher, the children race back and forth between two clearly defined markers. On the signal to stop, the runs scored are asked for.

Filling the basket   The teacher scatters a basket full of small balls over the play area. The children gather the balls and refill the basket as quickly as possible. The class may be divided into groups so that the groups may compete in the number of balls each returns to the basket.

Do this, do that   At the start of this activity, the children are told to imitate their teacher when she says, 'Do this', but to ignore the instruction, 'Do that'. As awareness increases, the pace of the game is speeded up.

Fishes in the net   Four or five children form a net by joining hands in a line. They then try to encircle other children who, when caught, become part of the net. As the net becomes unwieldy, it is divided into two nets. The winner is the last 'fish' uncaught.

Ships, lifeboats and aeroplanes   One end of the play area is designated 'Ships' and the other end 'Lifeboats'. When the teacher calls, 'Sail the ships' or 'Sail the lifeboats', the children rush to the appropriate end. At the call of 'Aeroplanes', they should stop and make themselves small, so as not to be seen from the air. The game intensifies as the teacher occasionally points to the lifeboats and, at the same time, calls 'Ships'.

Follow my leader   This is usually initiated by the teacher, who moves around the play area performing various activities with or without apparatus. The children follow, imitating these activities. As the pupils gain in experience, they are persuaded to take over the leader's role. The game can become a group activity, with a leader in each group.

Do as I do   This game is another version of 'follow my leader', but the activities do not need to be carried out on the move.

Catch your partner's tail (plate 8) The children work in pairs, with one running away and the other endeavouring to retain contact with his or her partner. The child running away wears a coloured braid tucked into the back of his or her shorts. If the chaser can acquire this tail by seizing it, the roles are reversed.

Games played without apparatus

Many of these games can be used as warm-up activities in the introductory part of the lesson, but a number have a rightful place in the third part, which is devoted to games. If they are not directly related to any other individual game, they have in common the requirements of space-finding, moving with safety, all-round vision and good observation.

Dodge and mark Children are arranged in pairs, as markers and dodgers. On a given signal, the dodgers attempt to escape the markers. The latter try to remain within reaching distance of their particular dodgers. On a whistle blast or the command 'Stop', all players immediately stand still. At this stage, the teacher asks how many markers can touch their dodgers. After a few attempts, the markers and dodgers change places.

Paddy says This is a slightly more advanced version of the infant game, 'Do this, do that'. The children are told that Paddy is a Sergeant-Major, who must always be obeyed. The teacher then proceeds to issue commands and instructions which should not be obeyed unless prefaced by 'Paddy says'.

British bulldog Two parallel lines are marked, one at either side of the playing area. The region outside these lines is regarded as the safe area and the class members, with the exception of a selected few, are placed in this region. The other pupils, singled out, are the catchers and remain in the central 'danger zone'. On a given signal, the runners must cross the danger zone to safety at the other side. If the catchers manage to lift a runner off the ground, this captive joins the catchers.

The game is repeated until the last pupil to avoid capture becomes the victor.

Chinese wall   This game combines the features of fishes in the net and British bulldog. It is played in the same way as British bulldog, but the catchers link hands to form a wall. The runners must either get round the wall or through it.

Prickly bear   This is a group game in which one child acts as a bear, sitting curled up in the centre of a chalked circle. The 'bear' has one defender, who tries to protect him from the light slaps of the other players. These players are only safe when they are outside the circle. If the defender catches one of these players within the circle, the captive becomes the bear, the bear becomes the defender and the defender joins the other players.

Poison   A pool of poison is represented by a large hoop or a chalked circle on the ground. Five or six players hold hands to form a circle around the danger area. Each player, by pulling and manoeuvring, endeavours to remain outside the poison, while forcing the other players into it.

Games involving ball-handling

Wandering ball   A group of children form a circle of about four metres radius, with one player inside the circle. The outside players pass a large ball back and forth across the circle, while the inside player endeavours to intercept these passes. If he or she is successful, the centre player changes places with the last thrower. This game can be adapted for rugby passing or for passing with the feet, soccer style.

Individual or circle dodge ball   Children are grouped in a circle, as for wandering ball and, again, with one player in the middle of the circle. The outside players try to hit the inside player below the knee with a large ball. He or she, in turn, tries to foil these attempts by dodging the ball. Any player who succeeds in scoring a hit changes places with the centre player. As skill increases, the outside players may resort to feint shots and passes to other players in more advantageous positions.

Team dodge ball   One team takes up its position inside a large circle or rectangle. The opposing team acts exactly as the outside players do in circle dodge ball, above. However, in this version, the targets are multiple. Points are scored for every hit recorded. After a time, the roles are reversed, the second period of the game being exactly the same length of time as the first. At the end of the second period, the team scores are compared and a winning team declared.

Defending the post or central pillar ball   Again, this is a group game with players spaced round the outside of a large circle. In the centre of the circle is a highjump stand or similar target. One player defends this target as the remaining players pass the ball and shoot at the post or pillar. A player scoring a successful hit changes places with the defender. The game can be adapted for soccer skill practice, but in this case a skittle should be substituted for the larger target.

Handball   Handball is an international game, played in many European countries and on the American continent. The rules are a little complex for many primary school children and the official goals are expensive to purchase or construct.

In the primary school, a simplified form of handball can be played, if space permits or if the playing area has blank walls at each end. In the latter case, goals are chalked rectangles about three metres long and sixty centimetres high, drawn about sixty centimetres above ground level. In an open space, two pairs of highjump stands bearing two horizontal parallel canes or ropes per pair form goals.

The game is played by two small teams on a rectangular area, approximating to one-third of a netball court. Players may dribble the ball and pass it, as described in the section on netball/basketball (see page 25) and shoot at the goals by throwing, one-handed. They are not allowed to carry the ball while moving.

A restraining arc of some three metres radius from the centre of each goal can be marked in chalk on the playground. Goals can only be scored from throws made outside this arc.

Ground handball This is a more popular version of the parent game, so far as the primary school is concerned.

In this game, the goals consist of benches turned on their sides so that their tops are turned inwards to face the court. In every other respect the court is the same as that for handball, which is described above. The ground handball court and the bench-type goals can also be used for shinty, crab football and the modified versions of soccer and hockey.

The ball is dribbled and passed, one-handed, along the ground. Shooting, again along the ground, is also executed one-handed.

As in all small-side team games, it is sound practice to have one team distinguished from the other by means of coloured braids.

Skittle ball or post ball The area required for this game approximates to one-third of a netball court.

The game is played by two small teams, each endeavouring to knock down a skittle at the opposing team's end of the court. The skittle is ringed by a large hoop or a chalk circle with a radius of about one metre, which acts as a restraining circle. Neither attackers nor defenders are allowed within it. Players are not permitted to carry or dribble the ball, but this encourages them to progress by passing the ball and then moving into an open space to receive a return pass. Plate 1 shows a game of skittle ball in progress.

Captain ball Two small teams play against each other on a court, similar to that used in ground handball. However, for captain ball, the benches are restored to their normal upright position.

49

One player from each side stands on the bench defended by the opposing team. This player has a similar function to that of the post in netball. In other words, if a player of his or her own team makes a successful pass to the player on the bench, from outside the restraining arc, and the ball is held on the bench for three seconds, a goal is scored. After each goal, the player on the bench is changed. Apart from the method of scoring, the game is played in every other respect exactly as skittle ball.

Newcombe and modified games of volleyball Two teams, ranging from one to six players per side, compete on a court of approximately eight metres by four metres. A net is stretched across the width of the court a little above head height. A light plastic football, size three or four, is played backwards and forwards across this net by the opposing players.

Points are scored by the team which 'grounds' the ball in its opponents' half of the court. Points are sacrificed by the team which plays the ball out of court.

Initially, players may catch the ball and then throw it to a partner or over the net. Later, rules can be introduced, preferably at the children's instigation, which will make the children play the ball in the manner described on page 27. In other words, they will use the front of the fists and lower forearms or the open fingers. Spiking may be introduced.

Eventually, correct serving is brought into the game and the players rotate their positions clockwise in each half of the court as a new session of serving is commenced.

Quoit tennis This is played in the same way as the early versions of Newcombe, in that the object is caught and thrown across a high net by opposing teams consisting of one or two players.

Although, strictly speaking, this is not a ball-handling game, it is so akin to games of the volleyball type that it fits this section. It might also be regarded as a close relative of tennis, since many of the throwing techniques and positions are similar to those required for forehand and backhand strokes in tennis.

Once more, points are scored by the team which grounds the quoit in its opponent's half of the court.

Gainings (throwing a ball)   Gainings is a suitable game for a wide open space or a field and can be played by two players, using a small ball or a rugby ball. One partner throws for distance and the other partner moves forwards or backwards to where the ball lands, in order to make the return throw. In the same way, the first player will position himself according to where the ball lands. In consequence, the partner achieving the greater average distance will eventually drive his partner backwards to a predetermined finishing line.

Murder ball   This is a small-side team game, usually associated with rugby. Murder ball should only be played on a soft grass surface.

Two teams oppose each other on a rectangular pitch some fifteen metres by eleven metres in size. Each team attempts to place a rugby or soccer ball by hand on a large mat or on an 'in goal area', marked at the opposing team's end of the pitch. Players pass the ball and run with it until they are held by the opposition. At this point, when no further play is possible, they must drop the ball. When a try is scored, i.e., when the ball is placed on the mat or target, the defending team takes possession of the ball.

Touch rugby   Touch rugby is not unlike murder ball, in that the ball is passed and eventually placed on a mat or goal area. The main difference lies in the fact that players are touched and not tackled by players of the opposing team. On being touched, the player in possession of the ball is obliged to pass it or drop it.

As skill develops, the pattern of passing backwards can be introduced.

Wild ball   A group of children is confined by a large chalked circle or rectangle. A plastic or light rubber ball is propelled within the area, one-handed, by the players. These players are allowed to strike the ball in this fashion, but they must not let the ball touch any other parts of their bodies. Each individual attempts to knock the ball against other players in the group.

Games involving kicking or striking a ball

Rebound tennis   A horizontal white line is painted or chalked on a wall, about one metre above ground level, to represent a net.

Two players, each having a padder tennis bat or play bat, play a ball alternately against the wall, aiming just above the net. A player scores a point when his or her partner fails to hit the ball as it leaves the wall or after one bounce on the ground. A point may also be scored if one player plays the ball at the wall below the white line.

Pat ball or modified fives   This game is played in exactly the same way as rebound tennis, but the open hand is used in place of the bat.

Modified tennis or padder tennis   Both tennis and padder tennis are official games, played on specified areas, with regulation equipment. These games can be played by two or four players on a rectangular court approximately ten metres by five metres. An improvised net is erected across the middle of the court at a height of about one metre.

Players attempt to hit the ball, using padder tennis bats or play bats, across the net and into their opponents' half of the court. Points are scored by a player or pair of players when the opposition fails to return the ball into the appropriate half of the court or allows the ball to bounce more than once on their own side of the net.

Hand tennis   Hand tennis is played as the above game is played, but hands are used instead of bats. The ball employed is usually of the light, beach ball variety. Played this way, the game is more suitable for younger children.

Tip and run This game is played in the same fashion as non-stop cricket, which is described on page 54. The only significant difference between tip and run and non-stop cricket is that, in the former game, a rounders bat or play bat is used in place of a cricket bat and the bowler's target is shoulder high.

Hot rice A child is given a cricket bat shape, play bat or rounders bat, with which to defend his or her legs. Other children in the group throw a medium-size plastic or rubber ball aiming to hit the defender below the knees. By pushing or knocking the ball away, the defending player can gain time to move away from the immediate vicinity of the ball. An attacker who scores a hit, picks up the bat, which the former defender must relinquish.

Soccer or heading tennis The game is played in exactly the same way as hand tennis, except that heads and feet are used in place of hands. The ball should be a plastic or rubber football. If a leather ball is used, it should only be partially inflated.

Teams may number from one to six per side. For the larger numbers, the court dimensions should be increased.

Five or six a side soccer The court is that already defined for ground handball and the game is played in the same way, although feet are substituted for hands.

If the ball goes out of court, a player of the non-offending team rolls the ball in immediately by hand. When a goal is scored, the defending side immediately takes possession of the ball. In this way there is an absolute minimum of time wasted. It may be necessary to impose penalties on players who kick the ball above knee height.

Crab football This is another version of five a side soccer and is played on the same court.

When playing the ball, the children must adopt the 'crab' position. This means that the body rests on the hands and feet, but is arched, with the chest uppermost. The hips may be lowered to a sitting position when not actually playing the ball. Again, the feet and possibly the head are used to propel the ball.

Gainings (kicking)   The game is played in the same way as laid down earlier (see page 51), but in this case the players drop a ball from their hands and employ a punt kick or drop kick to gain distance. Either a soccer or a rugby ball may be used. This should only be played on a field.

Non-stop cricket   An open space on a playground or field can accommodate this game. No boundary lines are necessary. The apparatus required consists of one set of playground stumps or actual cricket stumps, one skittle, one junior cricket bat or cricket bat shape, a small rubber ball and possibly a large hoop, with which to mark the bowler's circle.

The pitch is arranged as follows. The stumps are erected facing the bowler's circle, which may be six to nine metres away. A further wicket, to which the batsman will run, is established by placing a skittle about nine metres away from the stumps. This should be to the batsman's left as he stands in front of the stumps, facing the bowler's circle. If stumps are not available, two large skittles, a dustbin, or even one of the group baskets stood on end, may be substituted.

The two opposing sides should have five or six players each. One batsman stands in front of the wicket to defend it with the bat or cricket bat shape. The remaining batsmen stay behind a restraining line, a little way behind the batsman, so as not to interfere with play. The bowler takes up his position inside the circle, while the rest of his team adopt suitable fielding positions; these should include a wicket-keeper behind the stumps.

Every time he makes contact with the ball, the batsman is obliged to run to the skittle and back to the wicket, the completed return journey counting as one run. In the meantime, the bowler continues to bowl at the wicket, irrespective of whether the batsman is in a position to defend it or not. The fielders make their contribution by collecting the ball and returning it quickly and accurately to the bowler, who remains within his circle. When the latter hits the wicket, the batsman is out and must drop the bat. The incoming batsman must collect the bat and defend the wicket, before he too, is out. The sides change places when the last batsman is out. However, the change-over must be very rapid, as the new bowler begins bowling the moment he arrives in the circle.

At the end of an equal number of innings, or after a set period of time, the game ends and scores are compared. The question of whether or not batsmen should be out to catches should be resolved, jointly, by the players and the teacher. It may be influenced by the degree of difficulty experienced in dislodging the batting side.

As mentioned previously, this game can be adapted as a form of non-stop rounders.

Athletics or athletic games

A playground or field area can be utilised as an athletics arena. Obviously, when a grass area is available, the range of activities and games can be extended, and the availability of jumping pits can further increase this range.

Jumps If the construction of a pit is contemplated, a textbook dealing with drainage, materials and procedure should be consulted. However, so far as size is concerned, one which is approximately five metres by three metres may serve a dual purpose. High jump may be practised with an approach towards the long side of the pit and long jump from a longitudinal approach. Using this latter approach, children may also attempt the triple jump, known also as the hop, step and jump.

Where no pits are available, jumping should be limited to the standing broad jump on the grid, described on page 41 and shown in plate 9 and figure 7.

While it is sometimes useful and encouraging to the more

capable jumpers to know what height or distance they are achieving, in general, the points scoring system is more satisfactory for primary school children.

Running In competitive running, juniors can sprint, usually without discomfort, any distance between forty and eighty metres according to their age, physique and ability. A good compromise distance for a straight, uninterrupted run is sixty metres. Races of this kind should finish at a tape or when the runners cross a line marked on the ground, preferably between skittles or other markers. The children should not be asked to run towards a solid target, like a wall, in view of the obvious dangers!

As an alternative to sprints, there are relay races and hurdle races.

Not all schools are fortunate enough to have large enough open spaces to mark out standard athletics circuits. Consequently, relay races are more likely to be of the 'shuttle' variety, with participants running backwards and forwards along a straight course. One method of organising this kind of relay race is to divide the teams, placing equal numbers from each team at either end of the straight track. The first runner of each team runs to the opposite end of the track, crosses the line and starts the second runner by touching the latter's outstretched hand. This second child then runs along the track in the opposite direction to the first runner and starts the third runner in similar fashion. The process is repeated until the final runner crosses the finishing line. Alternatively, the runners may complete the return journey before handing on to their partners; this means that the starting and finishing lines coincide and all the runners start from the same end. Instead of touching hands, the runners may exchange relay batons.

There are many variations of relay racing. Obstacles may be introduced so that the children may be obliged to take a devious route. Participants may be expected to carry, pick up or set down objects, as in potato races and egg and spoon races.

8 Infant games: catch your partner's tail

9 *Standing broad jump: the points grid*

Balls may be introduced, which can be carried, thrown, dribbled by feet or hands or struck by an implement during the course of the race.

Hurdle races must be geared to the capabilities of all the participants and hurdles must therefore be low. Since hurdling is a form of running and not jumping, the hurdles for beginners may consist of canes or ropes, lying parallel to each other, at regular intervals along the ground. As the running across these hurdles becomes established, the canes may be gradually raised on wooden blocks or skittles. If the improvised highjump stands, consisting of canes in cement-filled tins are to be used as uprights, care must be taken to ensure that the hurdles are erected in the correct way. The horizontal canes should rest on the pegs in such a way that the runner who knocks one will dislodge it forwards, off the pegs. If the cane is on the oncoming runner's side of the upright, pressure against it will tend to push the stands over in the runner's path.

Throwing   Within the framework of a games period, there are obvious limitations on the choice of throwing events. There are the limitations of space, limitations in regard to safety and also limitations in respect of time, since a lot of time is wasted in the recovery of thrown objects.

The most suitable objects for throwing are balls and rubber quoits. All throwing should be executed from behind a clearly defined mark and should take place at a satisfactory distance from any other activity or obstacle. Early training in safety precautions is vital. All throwers should remain behind the throwing mark until the last individual has thrown. On a signal, all the throwers set out to retrieve whatever they have thrown and these are carried, not thrown, back to the mark. Throwing should not recommence until all the children are safely back behind this mark.

If possible, a series of concentric arcs should be marked to indicate distances from the throwing mark. A graded points scale should be related to these arcs, so that they can be utilised very much as the grid is in standing broad jump.

When a number of athletic events or games are taking place simultaneously, groups may rotate, collecting points at each event. In this respect, stop watches and measuring tapes can be used to assist in scoring, so long as more importance is attached to points than to measurements. A time of twelve seconds for the sprint event may be worth ten points, while thirteen seconds might score eight points. A team of five children may thus collect a joint score of forty-four points for this event and a joint score of forty-nine points for the next event, throwing the quoit. This type of scaled-down athletics competition between teams is sometimes referred to as 'potted sports'.

7 Specimen lessons

The following specimen lessons have been prepared with due regard to the area which is to be used, the time of year, the number of children involved and their age.

However, as has already been made very clear, not all children of a given age are capable of the same level of achievement. Local traditions in games may influence the areas in which children are strong or weak. For instance, certain regions are strongholds of rugby football. Here, many children are quite capable of handling a small rugby ball, even at the infant stage. Schools with excellent netball teams find that the younger children tend to imitate the practices of the older ones at every opportunity, with the result that a high standard of ball-handling is achieved in their early years.

For these reasons, it is recommended that the following examples should not be regarded as standard lessons for particular age groups, but merely as suggestions.

Specimen lesson – autumn term

CLASS	30 mixed infants, 5 and 6 years old
TIME	15 minutes
AREA	Playground
EQUIPMENT	6 baskets of small apparatus, including coloured braids
INTRODUCTION	Free play with small apparatus
	Scoring runs
	Catch partner's tail
CLASS ACTIVITY	Ball-bouncing practices, using medium-sized balls
	Throwing and catching the ball
GAMES	Crusts and crumbs
	Filling the basket
	Tag

Specimen lesson – spring term

CLASS	36 mixed infants, 5 and 6 years old
TIME	15 minutes
AREA	Playground
EQUIPMENT	6 baskets of small apparatus; hoops of various sizes; playground chalk
INTRODUCTION	Free play with small apparatus
	Free play with ropes or hoops
CLASS ACTIVITY	With a partner, throwing and catching a small ball
	With a partner, bouncing and catching a small ball
	Coaching aspect: Judgment of distance
GAME	Follow my leader (as a class or in groups)
	Wild ball (in groups)
	Paddy says

Specimen lesson – Summer Term

CLASS	36 mixed infants, 5 and 6 years old
AREA	Playground
TIME	15 minutes
EQUIPMENT	6 baskets of small apparatus; hoops
INTRODUCTION	Free play with small apparatus
	Exploratory work with bean bags or quoits
CLASS ACTIVITY	Experimental work with play bat and ball
	Partner activities, using bat and ball
	Coaching aspect: Watching the ball onto the bat
GAMES	Ships, lifeboats and aeroplanes
	Throwing bean bags into a hoop or circle

Specimen lesson – Autumn term

CLASS	30 mixed infants, 5 to 7 years old (vertical streaming or family groups)

TIME	20 minutes
AREA	Playground
EQUIPMENT	6 baskets of small apparatus
	1 large hoop
	Playground chalk
INTRODUCTION	Free play with small apparatus
	What time is it, Mr Wolf?
CLASS ACTIVITY	Experimental work with rubber or plastic balls
	Ways of bouncing balls
	Bouncing balls while on the move
	Coaching aspect: Awareness of environment and other players
GAMES	Group A: Knocking down skittles with bean bags
	Group B: Poison
	Group C: Tag
	Group D: Circle dodge ball
	Group E: Prickly bear
	Group F: Wild ball

Specimen lesson – Summer term

CLASS	36 mixed infants, 6 and 7 years old
TIME	20 minutes
AREA	Playground
EQUIPMENT	6 baskets of small apparatus
	36 assorted hoops
INTRODUCTION	Free play with small apparatus
	Experimental work with apparatus, other than balls
CLASS ACTIVITY	Exploratory work with hoops – how many ways can they be used?
	Practice with play bats and small balls, individually and in pairs

GAMES   Group A: Play bat and ball – rebound
                              scoring against a wall
                     Group B: Tag
                     Group C: Follow my leader
                     Group D: Low hurdle running
                     Group E: Throwing bean bags into a circle
                     Group F: Circle passing, using a medium-
                              sized ball

Specimen lesson – Autumn term

CLASS   40 mixed juniors, 7 and 8 years old
TIME   30 minutes
AREA   Large playground, having one netball court
                   and some additional space
EQUIPMENT   8 baskets of small apparatus
                   Playground chalk
INTRODUCTION   Free play with small apparatus
                   Free play with a different piece of apparatus
CLASS ACTIVITY   In pairs, passing and catching a rugby or
                   soccer ball
                   Repeat with two against one (pig in the
                   middle)
                      Coaching aspects: Reaching for the ball
                      and drawing it into the body. Finding
                      space to receive the ball
GAMES   Group A versus Group B: Skittle ball
                   Groups C and D: Wandering ball, using
                   soccer or rugby balls
                   Group E versus Group F: Ground handball
                   Group G versus Group H: Shinty

Specimen lesson – Summer term

CLASS   40 mixed juniors, 7 and 8 years old
TIME   30 minutes

AREA	Playing field with grass surface, with high jump pit available
EQUIPMENT	8 baskets of small apparatus 3 high jump stands 5 rounders posts, with targets 1 highjump bar, long rope or cane
INTRODUCTION	Free play with small apparatus Throwing and catching balls or bean bags, individually or in pairs
CLASS ACTIVITY	Groups A, B, C and D. In fours, using cricket bat shapes, skittles and small balls for practice of simple cricket skills (batting, bowling, fielding and wicketkeeping) Coaching aspect: Moving to the ball
	Groups E, F, G and H. In fours, using rounders posts with targets, play bats and small rubber or perforated plastic balls. Players alternately act as pitcher, striker, fielder and backstop Coaching aspects: Correct throwing and catching. Striking techniques
	After a short time, the two halves of the class exchange apparatus and activities
GAMES	Groups A and B: Non-stop cricket Groups C and D: Newcombe Groups E and F: Modified rounders Group G: High jump Group H: Defending the post

Specimen lesson – Autumn term

CLASS	36 mixed juniors, 9 and 10 years old
TIME	30 minutes
AREA	Playground with one netball court

EQUIPMENT	6 baskets of small apparatus
	2 netball posts
	4 rounders posts
	Long ropes for improvised nets
	Playground chalk
INTRODUCTION	Free play with small apparatus
	Free play with different apparatus
CLASS ACTIVITY	Boys: Soccer: in pairs, heading practice
	Soccer: in pairs, throwing in, heading and trapping
	Girls: Netball: in pairs, passing and then moving to take a return pass
	Coaching aspects: Moving to the ball. Passing with accuracy
GAMES	Group A versus Group B (girls): netball, played on one-third of the full court
	Group C (boys): heading tennis
	Group D (girls): quoit tennis
	Group E versus Group F (boys): handball

Specimen lesson – Spring term

CLASS	36 mixed juniors, 9 and 10 years old
TIME	30 minutes
AREA	One netball court on playground surface
EQUIPMENT	6 baskets of small apparatus
	1 pair of highjump stands
	2 benches
	8 pairs of skittles and/or improvised hurdles
	8 long canes
	4 rounders posts
	2 long ropes
	Playground chalk
INTRODUCTION	Free play with small apparatus
	Dodge and mark

CLASS ACTIVITY	Boys: 1 Soccer, passing in pairs
	2 Soccer, passing in threes, one against two
	Main coaching aspect: finding and using space

Girls: in pairs, using play bats and a ball for rebound practices against a wall
Main coaching aspect: footwork and body positioning

GAMES

Group A versus Group B (boys): soccer
Group C (boys): volleyball
Group D (girls): tennis
Group E (girls): hurdling
Group F (girls): circle dodge ball

Specimen lesson – Summer term

CLASS | 36 mixed juniors, 9 and 10 years old

TIME | 30 minutes

AREA | Playground and adjacent field with jumping pit

EQUIPMENT | 6 baskets of small apparatus
Assorted canes
3 improvised hurdles
1 pair of highjump stands
1 medicine ball
1 stopwatch or watch with sweep second hand

INTRODUCTION | Free practice with small apparatus
Jumping from one foot to discover correct take off foot
Jumping for height and jumping for distance

CLASS ACTIVITY | In pairs, relay baton changing
In pairs, highjump practices. One partner

65

kneels, holding out a cane, horizontally, while the other partner jumps over it

Coaching aspects: baton changing, while *both* runners are at speed; use of arms and good take off for jumps

ATHLETIC GAMES Group A: relay racing with baton changing three against three

Group B: hurdling

Group C: standing broad jump

Group D: high jump

Group E: potato race, using small balls as potatoes (a stopwatch is used to time this event)

Group F: shot putting, using a small medicine ball

8 Conclusion

In the foregoing chapters, a good deal of emphasis has been placed on the playing of small-side team games. The reader may have drawn the inference that national or large-size team games like soccer, hockey and cricket should not be attempted at primary school level, or that games of this type are harmful to younger children.

However, the authors do not subscribe to either of these views. Some children are quite capable of coping with the requirements of national games at an early age and many more children enjoy participating in them. Moreover, an immense contribution to the social education of children is given by those teachers who sacrifice their own time and energy to run school teams and to officiate during interschool fixtures.

What we do believe is that the national and major games provide opportunities for those with the necessary skill and should be regarded as supplementary to the more vital, basic games lesson dealt with in this book. Moreover, in the recommended lessons, the children are repeatedly taught the various enjoyable skills of the national games, and with greater experience of these skills comes more opportunity for success.

We sincerely hope that, having read the book many teachers will attempt to introduce and approach the teaching of games on the lines suggested. No doubt problems will arise and it is then that recourse to the local Physical Education Advisory Service may produce dividends. The Physical Education Adviser should be able to give advice on the provision of apparatus and the organisation of in-service training courses for teachers who are interested. The Adviser may also be able to arrange visits, so that teachers may see at first hand the type of work described.

This book will have achieved all that was intended if it can assist teachers to offer, through the medium of games in the primary school, enjoyment, exercise and opportunities for the acquisition of skill.

Bibliography

Other recent books dealing with primary school games include E Mauldon and H B Redfern's *Games Teaching* (Macdonald and Evans, 1969); W M Wise in *Games and Sports* (Heinemann, 1969), suggests useful progressions and the book is generously illustrated by simple diagrams. R M Lenel's book *Games in the Primary School* (University of London Press, 1969) explores the subject quite deeply and considers psychological aspects. F J M Johnson and M D Trevor, in their *Suggested Games Scheme for Juniors* (Blackwell, 1970) have taken the opposite approach and merely listed programmes for given age groups at different times of the school year. For those readers, who are particularly interested in the psychological basis of skill learning, this feature is ably dealt with by Dr H T A Whiting in *Acquiring Ball Skill* (G Bell and Sons Ltd, 1969). A chapter on infant games appears in W McD Cameron and M Cameron's *Education in Movement in the Infant School*, (Basil Blackwell, 1969).

The national governing bodies of sport supply rule books for the various games but a compendium of these rules, entitled *Official Rules of Sports and Games* is published by Kaye and Ward.

Simple, introductory coaching booklets, dealing with most games are included in the *Know the Game* series, published by Educational Productions Ltd.

Lists of books dealing with games and other aspects of Physical Education may be obtained from the regional offices of the Central Council of Physical Recreation or from the central office, 26 Park Crescent, London, W1N 4AJ. Similar lists are available from the Physical Education Association, Ling House, 10 Nottingham Place, London WM1 4AK.

Sources of Equipment

Most of the items of equipment mentioned in this book can, no doubt, be obtained in the reader's own locality, but for anyone who may have difficulty in doing so, the authors wish to offer the following suggestions. It should not be assumed that the suppliers listed are sole manufacturers or distributors of given types of equipment, although this may be so in connection with certain branded items.

Wire baskets, costing between £1·50 and £2·50 can be obtained from sports equipment suppliers but it is often economical to purchase them from wire manufacturers, like Sankey Green Wire Weaving Co Ltd, Thelwall, Warrington.

Playbats and Table tennis bats, ranging in price from approximately 10p to 150p are available from Grays of Cambridge, Playfair Works, P.O. Box 7, Cambridge; Slazengers Ltd, Challenge House, Mitcham Road, Croydon, Surrey; and Dunlop Sports Co Ltd, Allington House, 136–142 Victoria Street, London SW1. These manufacturers also offer a wide range of cricket bats, racquets, balls and other items suitable for playground games. Grays of Cambridge have recently added to their stock a short handled 'mini' racquet, ideally suited to young children.

Padder tennis equipment is available at approximately £11 per complete set from Slazengers, Grays of Cambridge and Lillywhites Contracts Ltd, 66 Battersea High Street, London SW 11. *Batinton sets* complete, at approximately £2·15, and *playground 'Flyback' stumps* at approximately £3·90, together with numerous other items of equipment, including *hoops*, can be obtained from Lillywhite Frowd Ltd, Medway Wharf Road, Tonbridge, Kent. Another supplier of general sports equipment is A G Spalding and Bros, Inc, Deodar Road, Putney, London, SW 15.

Moulded rubber balls, ranging in price from approximately £3 to £8, and many other kinds of balls are provided by Mitre Sports, Fitzwilliam Street, Huddersfield, by Slazengers and by Thomlinson of 450 Dumbarton Road, Glasgow.

Other suppliers of a wide variety of balls include Tonbridge Sports Industries Ltd, 28a Park Road, Southborough, Tunbridge Wells, Kent; A W Phillips Ltd, Nuneaton, Warwickshire, who supply coloured tennis balls; Webber Bros, Station Road, London, SE 25; Mettoy (Playcraft) Ltd, 5–6 Argyll Street, London, W 1, for plastic balls; Jabez Cliff, Walsall, Staffs; and P B Cow, (Lilo) Ltd, Lumley, Glasgow. Plastic or composition balls can be obtained from Surridge, Witham, Essex; and from Readers, Teston, Maidstone.

Skittles can usually be acquired locally or constructed from blocks of wood. However, a most useful and adaptable wire activity skittle, costing approximately 95p is available from Stephenson Arcade, Ltd, Chesterfield. These suppliers also deal with wire baskets, shinty sticks for about 45p, junior hockey sticks between £1·10 and £4·50 and slip catchers for cricket at approximately £5 or £10, according to type.

Finally, information on the *marking of pitches* for games is available in the form of an excellent wall chart, supplied by Sportsmark Ltd, Brentford, Middlesex at a cost of 40p.

Index